Rebound & the Bathtub

When your love refuses to go down the drain!

Flyer from the original production with the original cast. Top to
bottom: John D'Aquino, Lisa Soland, Jan Devereaux,
Glenn Swan, Gretchen Koerner, and Jeri Zucchi.

Rebound & the Bathtub

When your love refuses to go down the drain!

A Romantic Comedy

by Lisa Soland

All Original
Play Publishing

REBOUND & THE BATHTUB
Written by Lisa Soland
Copyright © 1998 by Lisa Soland

Published in 2024 by All Original Play Publishing
P.O. Box 32381
Knoxville, TN 37930
AllOriginalPlays@gmail.com

First Edition: April 2024
Printed in the United States of America
Graphic Design by All Original Play Publishing
Back cover photo by Steven L. Sears

ISBN: 978-1-956218-36-7
Library of Congress Control Number: 2024906386

Rebound & the Bathtub is dedicated to each and every person who helped bring the play to life!

"There is no destiny outside of what you give up or take on." – Dr. Laura Schlessinger

CAST of CHARACTERS

SARAH: A 35-year-old woman trying desperately to get out of her dysfunctional relationship.

LAUREN: Sarah's married friend who can only feel truly alive when living vicariously through someone else who seems to be having more fun than her.

DAVID: Sarah's boyfriend, in his mid-to-late 40s. He is a wishy-washy pathological liar whose charm can deceive even the audience.

JERRI: Sarah's best friend, level-headed and clear-thinking.

JANET: An aging actress in her 30s, a knockout but shallow.

LEE: A writer in his mid-to-late 30s, funny with a quick wit and good-looking in an average sort of way.

DIRK: Gorgeous but shallow, masculine, a player.

PLACE

SARAH'S studio apartment and neighborhood restaurants.

TIME

The present.

REBOUND & THE BATHTUB received its world premiere in The NoHo Theatre Festival at Theatre Unlimited in North Hollywood, California, on June 13, 1998. It was directed by Lisa Soland, produced by Rose's Name Game Productions, and Paul Hartel stage managed.

The cast was as follows:

SARAH .... Lisa Soland
LAUREN .... Jan Devereaux
JERRI .... Jeri Zucchi
JANET .... Gretchen Koerner
LEE .... Glenn Swan
DIRK .... John D'Aquino

A staged reading of the comedy was then presented at TU Studios on January 21, 2001, directed by Henry Polic II, produced by The Florida Project & Hilde Garcia, and stage managed by Garfield Mignott. *Sarah* was played by Lisa Soland, *Lauren* by Karesa McElheny, *David* by Lee Dawson, *Jerri* by Jeri Zucchi, *Janet* by Joanna Daniels, *Lee* by Chris Durmick, and *Dirk* by Scott Ford.

DESCRIPTION

Rebound & the Bathtub is a full-length romantic comedy about Sarah, our protagonist, who desperately tries to escape her dysfunctional relationship. When she follows the wacky advice of her closest friends, chaos abounds for all.

The play takes place in Sarah's studio apartment and various restaurants in town. It features four female and three male characters, each unique and chock-full of comical intrigue.

_____

It is a full-length play with an intermission and requires four females and three males.

- 4 f, 3 m -

REBOUND & THE BATHTUB

ACT ONE

Scene 1

SETTING: *We are in Sarah's studio apartment, where the*
            pullout couch, dresser, kitchen table, and two
            chairs are all in the same room. A bowl of
            fruit is on the table. Two other tables with
            their chairs are placed far downstage, right
            and left, or at other secondary locations in the
            theatre. These tables and chairs represent
            different restaurants that Sarah and Lee
            frequent.

AT RISE: *It is mid-morning, and SARAH and her*
            married friend LAUREN are having an
            intimate conversation.

SARAH: Only *you* would come up with an idea like that!

LAUREN: It's a good, solid idea, Sarah.

SARAH: Even if I were to consider it, I wouldn't know who
        to ask.

LAUREN: A friend. You ask a friend. A casual friend.

SARAH: *(After thinking briefly.)* There's this guy I've been
        having dinner with—

LAUREN: Uh huh...

SARAH: He's nice—a nice guy.

LAUREN: No! You can't make this kind of offer to a *nice* guy.

SARAH: Oh, so I'm supposed to ask some jerk?

LAUREN: No—a casual friend. Attractive, single, vital...
Hung like an ox.

SARAH: Do you share this side of you with your husband?

LAUREN: Where's your address book? Let's page through it
and see if it gives us any ideas.

SARAH: In the drawer, there.

LAUREN: *(Locating book, she pages through it.)*
Here we go. Paging... Paging... Dirk! Oh my God.
Dirk! God, was that easy or what?

SARAH: Dirk?

LAUREN: Ask Dirk. Dirk's a player. Ask a player.

SARAH: Yeah, but he's the type of guy I wouldn't want to be
with, you know? I went to the movies with him last
week, and...well. He's got a girlfriend, Lauren!
They've been together for—oh, I don't know—a
couple of years now. He's not single.

LAUREN: But is he hung like an ox? That is the question.

SARAH: Lauren!

LAUREN: He's got big feet, doesn't he?

SARAH: *(Correcting her use of language.)* He *has* big feet.

LAUREN: No, don't tell me. I can't stand it.

SARAH: I have no earthly idea how big his feet are. Why
would I be looking at his feet?

LAUREN: That's the first place I look.

SARAH: *(Restating what should be the primary concern.)*
He's not single!

LAUREN: He's not married. *(Beat.)* And he'd do it. That's my
point.

SARAH: But then I'm right back where I started, except worse. Dirk's worse than David. At least I know David's not going out with other women.

LAUREN: Oh, my dear innocent Sarah. When are you going to see the zucchinis in the patch?

SARAH: *(Sadly and quietly to self.)* Yeah.

LAUREN: *(Changing the subject.)* Listen, sweetie. Dirk is handsome, charming, and has a great...
(Makes motion of "great body.")
Hell, I'd do him. And then, what would be your end result?

SARAH: *(Quoting Lauren.)* "I would finally be able to cut myself free from this relation..."

LAUREN: *(Correcting her.)* Dysfunctional relationship.

SARAH: "Dysfunctional relationship."

LAUREN: Exactly.

SARAH: *(Thinking.)* Yeah. Well, thanks for the input.

LAUREN: Sure.

SARAH: You come up with some real doozies.

LAUREN: Well, there's always the alternative.

SARAH: And what's that?

LAUREN: Suffering. Writhing in pain. Wringing your guts out like a soiled washcloth. Calling out in your sleep. That is if you're able to sleep.

SARAH: Nope.

LAUREN: Can you eat?

SARAH: Nope.

LAUREN: You need to eat.

SARAH: *(Rises, crosses to table.)* Mother your children. I'm fine.

LAUREN: *You need to eat.*

SARAH: Oh, like I have some say in the matter. This is awful. Just awful. One would think that if you're in this much pain, it's better to stay in the relationship, so every time I go through this breaking-up process with him, I think to myself, "This really hurts. I'm in a lot of pain. Therefore, it must mean that we're meant to be together."

LAUREN: That ol' "Meant to be together" thing.

SARAH: So what do I do?

LAUREN: You get back together.

SARAH: Exactly.

LAUREN: Well, there you go. *(Beat.)* You keep getting back together to avoid the pain of breaking up.

SARAH: *(Realizing.)* You're exactly right.

LAUREN: Of course I'm right.

SARAH: And all you're saying is that there are other ways to avoid it.

LAUREN: All I'm saying is that if you can just lighten it a little, the pain, you might be able to dump this jerk.

SARAH: But how do you really feel about David? No, really. Don't hold back this time.

LAUREN: That's all I'm saying.

SARAH: *(Shaking her head.)* Only you would come up with an idea like this.

LAUREN: It's not bad. Not a bad idea. You ought to consider it.

SARAH: Want a banana or something?

LAUREN: You're changing the subject.

SARAH: *(SHE tosses LAUREN a banana from fruit bowl on kitchen table.)*
I could fix us some tea real quick?

LAUREN: *(She gathers her purse and rises.)*
> I've got to get going.
> *(Pealing banana.)*
> Jeffy's got the flu.
> *(Holding banana out for Sarah.)*
> You eat it. You should eat.

SARAH: *(Defending herself.)* I've been able to eat bananas.
> *(LAUREN steadfastly holds banana to feed starving Sarah. SARAH takes a quick bite to appease her.)*

LAUREN: *(Seductively.)* Well, now we know why.

SARAH: *(Mouth full.)* Very funny.

LAUREN: You addict.

SARAH: Thanks, Lauren.
> *(SARAH leads LAUREN to the front door.)*

LAUREN: *(Referring to the banana.)* Just think—that could have been Dirk.

SARAH: Time to go.

LAUREN: Think about it.

SARAH: *(Sarcastically.)* Oh, I will. I'm going to give that some real serious thought.
> *(She closes the door on Lauren.)*
> Not.

(Blackout.)

End of Scene

ACT ONE

Scene 2

AT RISE: *A while later, that same day. SARAH is in her apartment and hears something outside the front door. Before there is a knock, she crosses to door and opens it. DAVID is standing there, about to place a bunch of Sarah's belongings on her doorstep.*

SARAH: What are you doing?

DAVID: *(Placing items on doorstep.)*
      Returning some of your—

SARAH: I told you not to come up here.

DAVID: I know. I didn't see your car. I didn't think you were here.

SARAH: It's in the garage. I have a garage now *and* a bathtub.

DAVID: Oh. You have a bathtub?

SARAH: I said I did.
      (Pause.)
      Here, let me help you.
      (She takes some of the things from him.)

DAVID: Did you get my message?

SARAH: Yeah.

DAVID: Well?

SARAH: What? *(Defensively.)* I returned your call.

DAVID: What did you say?

SARAH: I said if you're going to drop off some things, drop off the new key as well.

DAVID: I left you three four-minute messages.

SARAH: Well, that's what I said.

DAVID: Oh. Well, no, then. I don't have the new key.

SARAH: David, why did you change the locks?

DAVID: Didn't I tell you?

SARAH: Why did you *really* change the locks?

DAVID: Oh. Well, that's why.

SARAH: I don't think so.

DAVID: Okay.

SARAH: I think you changed them because of me. Because of our arguing and my moving out.

DAVID: Why would I do that? Why would I then offer to give you a new key?

SARAH: *(Taking a breath, knowing she won't get the key.)* I have been trying to get you to change your locks for months. I've been telling you for months that your house sitter had been coming in when we weren't there. There were imprints on the bed, a woman's barrettes left under the pillow…

DAVID: *(Nodding his head.)* Yeah. Well, you were right. She came in again and watched that pay-per-movie channel. I found it on my bill, so—

SARAH: You changed the locks.

DAVID: Yes.

SARAH: Why couldn't you have changed them because I asked you to? I was living there too. I was paying you rent. Rent that practically covered your mortgage—

DAVID: *(Cutting her off.)* Is this what you want to talk about?

SARAH: *(Suddenly angry.)* I guess not. That's why I'm talking about it because I don't want to.

DAVID: Sarah, could you please tone it down—

SARAH: *(Suddenly calm and very direct.)*

Don't tell me how to be. Don't talk to me like that, with that condescending...thing. Don't ever talk to me like that again.

DAVID: Okay. *(Pause.)* Did you want to talk about all this now?

SARAH: Well, we're talking, aren't we?

DAVID: Yes, it's just that I've got to lock up my car if we're going to—

SARAH: *(Interrupting him.)* Well, go ahead. Lock it! Lock it up!

DAVID: *(Gingerly.)* Okay.

(He exits.)

SARAH: *(To self.)* Oh, God. Here we go again. This is that all-too-familiar conversation we have when he talks me, once again, back into this completely frustrating and suicidal relationship. Back into loving him. Back into sheer torture and hell...

(He enters.)

...hello.

DAVID: Hi.

SARAH: Hi.

DAVID: So—

SARAH: So what are we going to talk about?

DAVID: Well, the thing about the locks—

SARAH: Don't worry about it. I would just like a copy of the new key so I can get the rest of my stuff out *myself.*

DAVID: Okay, but it'll have to wait till Monday.

SARAH: Monday.

DAVID: Yes, Monday.

SARAH: *(Making sure she is more than clear.)*
I'll have a copy of your new key in my hand on Monday?

DAVID: Yes.

SARAH: That's fine.

DAVID: Fine.

(Blackout.)

End of Scene

ACT ONE

Scene 3

AT RISE: *The next day, mid-afternoon. SARAH and her best friend, JERRI, are sitting in her apartment.*

SARAH: I don't know what I'm going to do, Jare. I'm weak.

JERRI: You're not weak.

SARAH: I'm weak. Look at me.

JERRI: You have lost weight.

SARAH: I've been weak before.

JERRI: You are not weak!

SARAH: Are you sure it's not me?

JERRI: It's not you.

SARAH: Because I feel crazy. He makes me feel crazy.

JERRI: It's not you.

SARAH: God, I hate this. *(Beat.)* I'm a wreck.

JERRI: You know, I remember a Sarah who would not have put up with this crap for one split second.

SARAH: He hides my pictures, you know. Our pictures. I come home when he's not expecting me, and they're not in the front room anymore. He takes them down, and he places them into the study, where no one can see them—

JERRI: I know. You told me.

SARAH: *(Continuing.)* …and I come home unexpectedly and I say, "Who was here today?" And he says, "What?" And I say, "Who was here today? You've taken our pictures down again, and you've put them into the study."

JERRI: And what does he say?

SARAH: *(Defeated.)* Oh, you know. The same, ol' thing. It's always the same ol' thing.

JERRI: I'm sorry.

SARAH: What's happened to me, Jerri?

JERRI: I don't know.

SARAH: What happened to the strong me?

JERRI: She went to sleep.

SARAH: At least someone's sleeping around here. I've been up for three days.
(Rises and crosses to the kitchen to get a soda.)
Getting the rest of my stuff out of there has been gut-wrenching. No matter how thorough I am, he still finds something I've missed and has to bring it to me. He brings it to me! And if I don't catch him at the door, he leaves it there on my doorstep and doesn't knock, so I find it and know that he's been there…on my doorstep. What do they call that? Don't they call that passive-aggressive?

JERRI: You've been manipulated and played with too long.

SARAH: I mean, why doesn't he just knock? There's the door —just knock.
(From kitchen.)
Want a soda?

JERRI: No. *(Beat.)* You're going to have to not see him.

SARAH: *(Entering.)* Ohhh.

JERRI: *(Continuing.)* I'm not a therapist or anything, but if I was—

SARAH: Which you're not.

JERRI: If I was, I would say to take a good... Oh, I don't
know. What does Tony Robbins say about breaking a
habit?
(To self.)
Is it him who says that?
SARAH: Oh, so David's a habit now?
JERRI: Yes, it's him.
(To Sarah.)
"It takes 28 consecutive days to form a good habit or
break a bad one."
SARAH: Twenty-eight days?! Then why are you saying two
months? I could do 28 days. Twenty-eight days I
could do.
JERRI: Could you?
SARAH: Yes.
JERRI: Well, let's do one extra for good measure.
SARAH: I could do 28 days.
JERRI: *(She's found the solution.)* A good two months off and
not see him. Not talk to him.
SARAH: Don't I get any credit for moving out?
JERRI: No.
SARAH: I moved out.
JERRI: Yes, you did.
SARAH: *(Quickly changing subject.)* Did you notice my new
placemats? My sister made these from the photos
taken at my mom and dad's 45th wedding anniversary.
See this? This is my parents' home off the coast of
Seattle.
JERRI: You're not listening to me, are you?
SARAH: This is the view off their porch. This is the ocean,
Jare. This is the freakin' Atlantic Ocean.

JERRI: Actually, I think that's the freakin' Pacific Ocean.

SARAH: And they don't even live there full time. It's their "whenever" home. I could be there right now. I could be in "whenever," and then I could get the objectivity you and Mr. Robbins are talking about. Then I could let go.

JERRI: *(Doubtful.)* You said that about moving out.

SARAH: Yeah, you're probably right. I'd be on the phone calling him, "David, please come see me. I miss you so!"

JERRI: You're funny, makin' fun of yourself.

SARAH: Well, that's what I do.

(Pause.)

JERRI: *(Focusing.)* So, what is it? Why can't you let go?

SARAH: I don't know. My friend Lauren says it's the pain.

JERRI: Go deeper.

SARAH: Deeper than pain?

JERRI: *(Moving in.)* What are you afraid of?

SARAH: *(Thinking.)* Maybe afraid of being by myself, but that sounds so simple. I mean, you spend so much time with someone.

JERRI: *(Continuing to make her point, SHE finishes Sarah's sentence.)*

…that it becomes a habit.

SARAH: Eighty percent of it's great.

(JERRI gives her a look.)

Really. We talk about stuff.

JERRI: Stuff?

SARAH: I love to bounce things off of him. Other guys I've been with don't seem to bounce.

JERRI: Stuff.

SARAH: We talk constantly from the moment we see each other 'till we make love or fall asleep—

JERRI: *(Getting it.)* That's it!

SARAH: What did I say?

JERRI: You said, "Make love." You're sexually addicted.

SARAH: No. *(Beat.)* I don't think so. *(Beat.)* Really?

JERRI: *(Second big solution.)* You need to be alone, Sarah. Two months.

SARAH: Jerri.

JERRI: You do.

SARAH: I can't do two months, I'm telling you. I need the touch. I need the human contact thing. I need—

JERRI: You need two months alone.

SARAH: *(Moaning.)* Oh.

JERRI: Objectivity.

SARAH: Ohh.

JERRI: Tony Robbins.

SARAH: Ohhh.

JERRI: Yup.

SARAH: Listen to me moaning here. With moans like this, who needs David.

JERRI: That's the spirit!

SARAH: *(Quickly defeated.)* I can't do it.

JERRI: I don't know what to say.

(Blackout.)

End of Scene

ACT ONE

Scene 4

AT RISE: *The next day. SARAH and JANET are sitting*
                 on white iron chairs by a small table set up in
                 the DSL playing area. THEY are eating frozen
                 yogurt at their regular yogurt shop.

SARAH: I've decided that relationships suck. That's what I've
          decided. Actually, that's not entirely true. Life is what
          sucks. Life is really sucky.

JANET: Yeah.

SARAH: I was talking with my friend Jerri, and she's married.
          She's in a really good relationship—not because she's
          married—that's not what I mean. She's just in a really
          good relationship, married or not.
          (Beat.)
          Her husband's a good man. He respects her, treats her
          good. Stuff like that.

JANET: Yeah.

SARAH: And she was like telling me that... Well, they're
          going through a really hard time right now and
          well...she's sick of him. Yeah, know? He's driving her
          crazy. She can't stand to be around him.

JANET: Yeah?

SARAH: I mean, I guess couples go through that.

JANET: Oh, yeah.

SARAH: My younger brother's wife tells me that they go
          through stuff like that all the time. And they have a

good relationship too. I mean, I know that they will be together for the duration.

(Beat.)

They talk. They communicate, and well…she kicked out the windshield of his truck one time. He was pissing her off, and she just kicked it right out from the inside.

JANET: Did insurance pay for that?

SARAH: Yeah. They made up this story about how they had hit a deer on the freeway and thought it was dead, so they dragged it over to the car and somehow lifted it up into the cab. Started off driving again, and then suddenly the deer came back to life and started freakin' out.

JANET: Wow. Some deer.

SARAH: It's a made-up story.

JANET: Right. Right.

SARAH: *(Continuing.)* So, they said it started to go crazy on them, maybe from being in such a small, restricted area, and it just…butted its head into the front window until they stopped the truck and set it free.

JANET: Why didn't they just say a rock hit their windshield?

SARAH: I don't know. I guess they were covered in the natural disaster area or something. Insurance wise.

JANET: A rock is a natural disaster.

SARAH: I don't know.

JANET: Jeez.

SARAH: But my brother can drive her crazy and visa versa, I suppose.

JANET: Yeah.

SARAH: My friend Jerri says that life is hard when you're not
in a relationship, and life is hard when you're in one.
JANET: Maybe life's just hard.
SARAH: That's what I'm thinking.

(Blackout.)

End of Scene

ACT ONE

Scene 5

AT RISE: *As the lights come up we see SARAH at the*
        front door with DAVID standing just outside,
        holding more items.

SARAH: More stuff, huh?

DAVID: Yes.

SARAH: Didn't I tell you not to worry about anything I might
        have missed and that I'd get it?

DAVID: Yes you did, but—

SARAH: You didn't see my car.

DAVID: Yes. I'm sorry. Should I come back—?

SARAH: No! Let me help you.
        (She takes an arm full of stuff from him.)
        No key?

DAVID: No, not yet.

SARAH: Is it Monday, or is it just me?

DAVID: Is that your piece of wood on top of my Pac Man
        machine?

SARAH: What?
        (Beat.)
        Oh. Does it have little holes punched into it?

DAVID: Yes.

SARAH: I can't believe I forgot that. That's my aggravation
        board game. Did you see a bag of marbles up there,
        too? Antique marbles? Hopefully?

DAVID: Uhm. I'm not sure.

18

SARAH: My dad made that for me. Drilled all the little holes into it by hand.

(Beat.)

It's a game.

DAVID: Yes.

SARAH: You knew that?

DAVID: No. I'm just trying to be agreeable.

(THEY finish carrying in the stuff.)

SARAH: Thanks for bringing this up.

DAVID: When are we going to talk?

SARAH: *(A big breath.)* I think it would be a good idea if we took some time apart.

DAVID: Oh, really?

(Beat.)

Okay.

SARAH: Like, maybe two months or something like that.

DAVID: Oh.

SARAH: I'm really confused and angry—

DAVID: Well, you're not alone.

SARAH: What do you have to be angry about?!

DAVID: *(Angry and ugly.)* It's my phone messages you listened to. I think that's pretty awful, Sarah.

SARAH: Well…

(A forced smile.)

What can I say?

DAVID: *(Back to charming.)* Anyway, I'm sorry I didn't get up here earlier. I had to go down to DWP to keep them from shutting off my water.

SARAH: Hmm. You're life's a mess.

DAVID: *(Angrily.)* Well, thank you, Sarah. Thank you very much.

(Turns and walks away.)

(Blackout.)

End of Scene

ACT ONE

Scene 6

AT RISE: *Another small table placed in the DSR playing area. It represents a nice restaurant where SARAH and her male friend LEE now sit. THEY are holding menus and are mid-conversation. LEE is wearing his usual baseball cap backward.*

LEE: That's what I did with you.

SARAH: *(Surprised.)* You did?

LEE: Oh, yeah. When I found out you had a boyfriend, I totally backed down.

SARAH: Really?

LEE: Oh yeah. *(Beat.)* I was interested in you.

SARAH: You were?

     (LEE nods.)

     That's nice to hear.

     (Beat.)

     I mean, I'm glad you told me because a lot of people wouldn't... I mean, a person thinks things but... Well, anyway, thanks for telling me...that.

LEE: So I can understand this guy doing that. When I heard, I just switched it off and started thinking, "Friendship."

SARAH: Friendship.

LEE: "Friendship."

SARAH: That's good. We can do friendship. That's actually what I was thinking.

21

LEE: Good.

   (Beat.)

SARAH: So now finish that story.

LEE: Which one?

SARAH: That one you were telling me before I told you that one about that guy asking me out.

LEE: The dorm one?

SARAH: Yeah.

LEE: Okay. Well, we were studying. Like I told you. Calculus, I think it was. Like I cared about calculus. I was an English major. I wasn't going to write books about math.

SARAH: Right.

LEE: But I guess I was better at it than she was…

   (Beat.)

   Actually, I tutored a great deal of people, now that I think of it.

   (Beat.)

   Anyway, she said she had to take a shower, and I thought, "No big deal. I'll just keep working." About ten minutes later she comes back in and sits down next to me on the bed.

SARAH: Those twin-sized ones, right?

LEE: Yeah, it's college. They think you're the only one who's ever gonna be lying in it.

SARAH: Right.

LEE: Which practically was the case with me, to be honest with you.

SARAH: Hmm.

LEE: She sits there and we begin studying again only the
      next thing I know, she's accidentally dropped the
      towel.
SARAH: Accidentally?
LEE: Yeah.
SARAH: *(Doubtful.)* Right.
LEE: What?
SARAH: Women do not "accidentally" drop towels. Okay? It
      ain't done. If a towel drops, it's in accordance with her
      "direct-and-carefully-thought-out plan."
LEE: Okay. Anyway, so I was sitting there—
SARAH: *(Continuing.)* When I wear anything that's as little as
      a towel and I know that there's nothing underneath—
LEE: *(Interested.)* Yeah?
SARAH: Like a bikini. When I wear a bikini, I put double-
      sided tape around every inch of my...uh...
LEE: What?
SARAH: You know.
LEE: No, I don't.
SARAH: The bodice part. Around my bodice. Part.
LEE: Right. Anyway, listen—
SARAH: Sorry. I interrupted you.
LEE: Okay, so I'm sitting there, and I notice that the towel has
      accidentally...
      (Beat.)
      The towel is now lying on the bed. Okay? It's lying
      there.
SARAH: Fine.
LEE: She sees me notice that the towel is no longer serving its
      old purpose, so she gets up and turns off the light.
SARAH: Jeez.

LEE: I feel her coming near me, and I'm thinkin', "What am I gonna do?"

SARAH: *(Nodding.)* Right... Right...

LEE: She gets onto the bed—

SARAH: Those skinny college dorm ones—

LEE: ...right alongside of me and starts literally engulfing me, surrounding me with kisses and arms moving all over the place and I felt so stupid.

SARAH: Why?

LEE: Because I didn't like it. I didn't feel... Well, I felt like she wasn't taking me seriously. Like when tomorrow came, this whole event would have meant nothing to her.

SARAH: *(Surprised.)* Really?

LEE: Yeah. So I took her by the wrist, walked her over to the light switch, turned it back on, and sat her down on the bed.

SARAH: Was she still...uh...naked at this point?

LEE: Oh, yeah. Completely. Nice breasts, too.

SARAH: Lee!!!

> *(SARAH glances around the restaurant to make sure no one is overhearing them.)*

LEE: Well, I'm telling you.

SARAH: Okay.

LEE: *(Becoming more direct, almost as though he is talking directly to SARAH.)*

Anyway, I picked up the towel and I placed it over her and I said, "I know what you're doing here. I'm not stupid. I know what's going on. You women think you have the patent on intuition, but I understand. And when you're out of this relationship you're in, when you're completely out of it, then we'll talk."

SARAH: Wow.

LEE: *(Breaking the spell.)* That's what I said to her. I looked her right in the eye and told her that.

SARAH: Good for you.

LEE: I guess.

SARAH: Did you ever see her again?

LEE: Oh, sure. She finally broke up with the guy, and we dated for two years. Till I moved out here and she stayed, for reasons of her own.

SARAH: That's great, Lee.

LEE: Yeah.

SARAH: Hmmm.

LEE: I like that sort of thing. You know? The direct approach.

SARAH: That's great. Very impactful.

(Blackout.)

End of Scene

ACT ONE

Scene 7

AT RISE: *We are back in SARAH'S studio apartment*
           with her friend, JERRI.

JERRI: So, how's it going?

SARAH: *(Attempt at cheery.)* It's okay.

JERRI: Is it?

SARAH: *(Plainly.)* No. You know. It sucks.

JERRI: Sorry.

SARAH: It's okay.

> *(Beat.)*

> I get to the point with him when my body just can't hold any more pain. Ya' know?

JERRI: You shouldn't have to.

SARAH: If I could just cry. If I could just have a good cry.

JERRI: I think you've been doing a lot of that.

SARAH: Yeah, but it's not the right kind of crying. It's been, "Crap, I'm in a lot of pain, and I can't get rid of this," kind of crying. It hasn't been the "I see the light at the end of the tunnel" sort. That's what I need—the tunnel sort.

> *(Beat.)*

> I'm in the pre-tunnel stages.

JERRI: A good release.

SARAH: I need a good release. Something to release me.

> *(Beat.)*

I've been having a lot of problems with my
abdominals.

JERRI: Abdominals? Your stomach muscles? Is that what you
mean?

SARAH: No. Uhhh. The inside. Pain in my gut. Down here.

JERRI: Abdomin.

SARAH: Right. Right.

JERRI: How long has that been going on?

SARAH: Three years.

JERRI: How long have you been dating David?

SARAH: Three years.

JERRI: You need to listen to your body.

SARAH: I wish I could just throw it all up. Just throw it up.

JERRI: Have you considered therapy?

SARAH: Thanks, Jare.

JERRI: I'm serious.

SARAH: I know you are.

JERRI: Well?

SARAH: We went, you know. As a couple. Off and on.

JERRI: What did your counselor say?

SARAH: *(Beat.)* I'm actually really angry about that, too.

JERRI: Really?

SARAH: Yeah. He said that there is no right or wrong. That
there's just people and opinions.
(Grasping for hope.)
But Jare, there is right and wrong. Isn't there?

JERRI: Definitely.

SARAH: I mean, like that foreigner who found out his wife
was having an affair, so he killed her and their five
children. That's wrong!

JERRI: Not if you live in Iraq. They can do that over there.

SARAH: *(Strongly.)* Well, this is America. Okay? We're in freakin' America. And there is right and wrong here. *(Beat.)* When you're in a relationship it's wrong to make a promise to not do what you know would definitely upset your mate and then…do it anyway. To break a promise. And then to lie. That's wrong.

JERRI: I agree.

SARAH: *(Weak again.)* I mean, is it me?

JERRI: No.

SARAH: Okay. I just don't think he has healthy boundaries. That's all.

(Lowers head into her hands.)

JERRI: Oh, he's got 'em. The fence just don't go around you.

SARAH: *(Looking up.)* Yeah.

(Blackout.)

End of Scene

ACT ONE

Scene 8

AT RISE: *A different restaurant but the same DSR table.*
                 LEE and SARAH are holding different menus.

LEE: The waiter asked me if this was our second date or our
        third.

SARAH: What did you tell him?

LEE: I told him you were a prostitute.

SARAH: Thank you very much.

LEE: He said he wanted your number.

SARAH: Thanks, Lee.

LEE: Sure. That's what friends are for.

SARAH: Lee?

LEE: Yeah?

SARAH: Can I ask you a rhetorical question?

LEE: Sure. Rhetoric away.

SARAH: Let's say two people are living together—a guy and
        a girl.

LEE: Is this a gay guy and a straight girl or a straight guy and
        a straight...? What I'm asking is if these two
        rhetorical people are romantically involved?

SARAH: Yes. Yes, they are. Let's say that rhetorically they
        are.

LEE: Okay.

SARAH: Do you think it's kind of strange if one person
        doesn't let the other person answer his or her phone?

LEE: They're living in the same house?

SARAH: Yeah. Together. Romantically.

LEE: What do you think, Sarah?

> *(Beat.)*
>
> I mean, if this was you, what would you think about that?

SARAH: I wouldn't feel very good about that.

LEE: Me neither.

SARAH: Yeah.

> *(THEY go back to the menus.)*
>
> Lee?

LEE: Yeah?

SARAH: Do you ever eat alone?

LEE: Me?!

SARAH: Yeah.

LEE: *(Lying.)* Nooo.

> *(SARAH smiles.)*

SARAH: So, what are you ordering?

LEE: Oh, same.

SARAH: What's the same?

LEE: Steak. New York. Medium rare.

SARAH: Sounds good.

LEE: *(Raising an arm.)* Waiter!

SARAH: *(Stopping him.)* No, I mean, that sounds good for you. I haven't decided yet.

LEE: Oh.

SARAH: I used to be really good at important decisions—life-altering ones—but the simple ones were impossible. Now, I'm just as bad at both.

LEE: Take your time.

SARAH: Thanks.

LEE: So, what did you do today?

SARAH: Don't talk to me, okay? Let me just concentrate on
        this menu here.
LEE: Okay.
        (Long silence.)
SARAH: Okay, got it.
LEE: Great. Waiter!
        (Raises arm.)

        (Blackout.)

End of Scene

ACT ONE

Scene 9

AT RISE: *SARAH and JANET are sitting at the DSL table, once again eating yogurt.*

JANET: So what do you think?

SARAH: *(Excited.)* Great. I think he's great. I want you to meet him.

JANET: Me? *You.* He's for *you*, Sarah.

SARAH: No. No. *(Lee's just a friend.)* I'm not in a place to... I'm in a relationship, remember?

JANET: *(Slightly sarcastic.)* Oh, yeah. Right.

(Beat.)

Well, describe him to me.

SARAH: He's funny. Really funny. A quick wit.

JANET: And he's a writer?

SARAH: Yeah.

JANET: Is he the kind of writer who has to be witty all the time? Like...can't turn it off type-of-writer?

SARAH: No, he's not a typewriter.

JANET: Oh.

SARAH: And he's strong, Janet. Really strong and smart and settled in life.

JANET: What does he look like?

SARAH: Ohhh. I don't know.

JANET: Is his hair growing thin? Is he balding?

SARAH: *(Thinking.)* Actually, yes. I guess it is.

JANET: I don't like balding men. There's a vulnerability to
       them that reminds me of my cellulite.

SARAH: Jeez, Janet. I don't know. Maybe it's just receding a
       little. Do you want to meet him or not?

JANET: *(Setting down her yogurt.)* Sure. I just don't want him
       to know that I'm meeting him, meeting him.

SARAH: *(Picking up Janet's yogurt and finishing it.)*
       Okay. I can arrange a non-arranged meeting.

JANET: Make it like an accident. Like we just happened to
       run into each other.

SARAH: *(Remember the conversation with Lee.)*
       An accident, huh?

JANET: Yeah.

SARAH: A "direct-and-carefully-thought-out-plan?"

JANET: Yeah.

(Blackout.)

End of Scene

33

ACT ONE

Scene 10

AT RISE: *Back in Sarah's apartment, DAVID and SARAH are sitting on the sofa, mid-conversation. More of Sarah's returned items are scattered about their feet.*

DAVID: I'm just saying that you shouldn't have listened to my messages.

SARAH: Well, you shouldn't have given me reasons to listen to them.

DAVID: All right. *(Beat.)* Sarah, it's wrong to listen to another person's messages.

SARAH: I thought there was no right and wrong, only each other and what makes us feel safe.

DAVID: You're safe.

SARAH: David, I'm really clear about what I want now. I'm 35, and I'm really clear. I want to get married. I want to have the option of raising a healthy and happy family. I want to be able to live with someone and share the same phone!

DAVID: I never answered your phone or listened to your messages.

SARAH: But you could have. That's the difference.

DAVID: I have at least 20 to 30 calls coming in each day. Important calls. If you're answering my phone, then I'm not going to get those messages.

SARAH: I have taken messages for you, and you got them.

DAVID: Yes, but I told you not to answer my phone and you
    did anyway.

SARAH: Why is it such a big deal?! It should not be such a
    big freakin' deal.

    (Pause.)

    I'm psychic. Did you know that? And when you lie to
    me I know it.

DAVID: What's that supposed to mean?

SARAH: *(Dead serious.)* It means let's quit with the lying.

DAVID: I don't lie.

SARAH: Yes, you do. We've already decided that. You just
    said that you should have talked with me first before
    you called her.

DAVID: And I'm sorry. I said I was sorry.

SARAH: So you lied.

DAVID: Okay, I lied.

SARAH: You broke a promise.

    (Pause.)

    I know that was her that night when I answered the
    phone.

DAVID: *(Dismissing.)* Oh, you mean the one that hung up?

SARAH: No, I do not mean the one that hung up. This one
    called, and I said, "Hello?" She said, "Oh. Is David
    there?" I said no. She said, "Oh, is he coaching
    tonight?" I said, "Yes. Can I take a message?" "No,
    that's okay. I'm just returning his call. I'll call back
    later." And I thought, "I know that voice. I know that
    voice very well."

DAVID: You shouldn't have answered it.

SARAH: I should be able to.

    (Beat.)

Why did you have to call her? Why can't you just let it go?

DAVID: I told you why.

SARAH: Did you think about me when you called her? Did you think about our agreement?

DAVID: Sarah, you and I made that agreement a long time ago, and I have been feeling lately that there's no longer any need for that agreement. She was in a really bad place back then and she's not now. She's got a boyfriend, I guess.

SARAH: *(Under breath.)* You always say that. You always say they're married, or they have a boyfriend, or they're a Mormon—

DAVID: *(Continuing.)* Last I heard, she was moving to Alaska with him or something—

SARAH: *(To self.)* Oh, "Alaska." That's a new one.

DAVID: See?

SARAH: Is that supposed to make me feel better? Alaska?

DAVID: I don't even know what's going on in her life.

SARAH: Why couldn't you leave it that way?

(Beat.)

DAVID: You know, Sarah, if you weren't in my life if I were alone, I wouldn't be doing anything differently.

SARAH: Yes, I know.

DAVID: *(Continuing.)* I wouldn't suddenly call her or any other woman for that matter and say, "Hey, let's go out. I'm a free man!"

SARAH: I know that.

DAVID: I don't do these things because you ask me not to.

SARAH: I know.

DAVID: So what's the problem?

SARAH: I just wish... I just wish you would.

(Blackout.)

End of Scene

ACT ONE

Scene 11

AT RISE: *SARAH and LEE are at a Sushi restaurant, same table, DSR. Although this appears to be a fine dining restaurant, LEE wears the usual baseball cap, backwards.*

SARAH: *(Setting down the menu down.)* I hate restaurant food. I'm tired of eating out.

LEE: Okay. Let's look at our options.

SARAH: *(Rising.)* Eating in! How's that for an option?!
    (Gathering purse.)
    Let's get out of here.

LEE: Oh, and that would look real good. "Hey Sarah, come on over to my bachelor pad, and we'll slowly cook us up some tenderloins on my hot, sizzling grill."

SARAH: *(Quickly.)* Sounds delicious. Let's go.

LEE: *(Rising, HE stops her.)* I don't think so.
    (SARAH sits. LEE sits. THEY go back to the menus.)

SARAH: Lee?

LEE: Yeah?

SARAH: Never mind.

LEE: What?

SARAH: Do you think you'll ever marry again?

LEE: Yeah, sure. Why not.

SARAH: *(Surprised.)* Really?

LEE: Oh, yeah. My first marriage was a mistake.
    (Beat.)

I know they all say that, but mine really was a
mistake. I thought she was somebody else.

SARAH: That's easy to do. We've all gotten involved with
people we don't know very well at first, and by the
time we do, it's too late because we're addicted in one
way or another.

LEE: You don't understand. Susan was a very interesting
woman. There was much I didn't know about her, the
first of which was that she had a lot of boyfriends.
Lots. Like cattle, lots. And she couldn't tell them
goodbye. Like a vegetarian, she couldn't send them to
the slaughterhouse. Second of which, she had a twin
sister named Cindy. Now Cindy was sweet. Nice girl,
but that's not the point. Susan ran away with Peter and
sent her twin sister to the church to marry me.

SARAH: No way. You're joking. Right?

LEE: I walked through the entire ceremony thinking that this
was the woman I met at Disneyland.

SARAH: *(Now in total disbelief.)* You met your ex-wife at
Disneyland?!

LEE: Yeah.

SARAH: Never marry a woman you meet at Disneyland.

LEE: Where I met her was not the problem.

SARAH: *(Continuing.)* It's just such a happy, magical place. I
mean, the castle alone, all that Sleeping Beauty crap.
That never happens. I don't know anyone in my life
who has ever had that happen. And they never go into
a "coma," which is probably what really happens.
They go into "a deep sleep." Doesn't that sound
romantic? "A deep sleep?" If that ever happened to
me, if I ever woke up and had some gorgeous, dragon-

killing guy kissing me, I would definitely know that it was all a dream. Life just ain't like that. I mean, it's like marrying Minnie Mouse, for God's sake—plastic, polka dots, and lace. There's just no way a couple can pull through all that delightful, tender happiness and survive. It's the day-to-day stuff that counts. Eating. Now eating counts!!!

LEE: Can I continue?

SARAH: Sorry.

LEE: Anyway, I stood at the altar saying my vows to Cindy thinking all along that she was the woman I let talk me into bungee jumping off of Pike's Peak. Little did I know she was off jumping onto Peter's peak.

SARAH: You've got to be joking. How can you joke about something like that?!

LEE: This is life. Or I should say, "This is my life." It's not fair to suggest that this kind of thing can happen to just anyone.

SARAH: Why didn't you get an annulment?

LEE: I tried. But she sent Cindy to do that, too, so the signature was default…again.

SARAH: Jeez.

LEE: It took three times, three visits to city hall, and by then, too much time had passed. Cindy was thrown into prison for forgery. I visited her a couple of times, which makes me an idiot, doesn't it?

SARAH: No.

LEE: Chocolate chip cookies and everything. I have a history of attracting dysfunctional women. Accidents all over the place. I just invite them into my life. Have a sit.

Stay a while. Sure, why not. I realized one day who
the common denominator was.

SARAH: Who?

LEE: Me. 'Cause when you got one finger pointed out, there's
always three pointing right back at ya'.

(JANET approaches their table.)

JANET: *(Play acting.)* Sarah! Hey, what are you doing here?!

SARAH: *(Rising and hugging her.)* Hey, hi. What's going on?

JANET: Oh, nothing. What an accident running into you here.
I was just stopping by to...

(Bitingly sarcastic.)

Well, you know me. I love Sushi. Raw fish. Yum. My
favorite.

SARAH: Oh, excuse me. Janet, this is Lee. Lee, this is my
friend, Janet.

LEE: *(Standing to make a proper greeting.)* Hi. It's nice to
meet—

JANET: *(Quickly, without kindness.)* Hi. How ya' doing?
*(Turning her back to Lee, thinking it will elicit his
interest. She talks directly to Sarah.)*
You're never going to believe this. I had a dream
about you last night.
(LEE sits.)

SARAH: *(Mock chuckling.)* Oh, you and your dreams.

JANET: We were on a bed together—you, me, and some guy.
(Glancing back at Lee.)
Uhhh... George, I think it was. George. I mean, we
weren't doing anything or anything. We were just
rolling around and laughing. Telling jokes.

LEE: Interesting.
(Rising again.)

Would you like to join us?

JANET: Oh, sure. Thank you.

> *(JANET sits. SARAH crosses between Janet and Lee on her way to get a third chair. JANET rises.)*

Oh, wait. I shouldn't be interrupting.

SARAH: No, it's okay.

LEE: We do this all the time.

SARAH: *(Explaining to Janet.)* Well, not all the time, all the time.

LEE: *(To Janet.)* You look familiar. Have we met?

JANET: *(Intimately.)* No, I think that's something I would definitely remember.

SARAH: *(To self.)* Oh, God.

> *(Exits DSR.)*

LEE: I'm sure of it. Are you an actress, by chance?

JANET: Actually, yes. Yes, I am.

LEE: Oh, I got it! "Slippery Seaweed Runs Deep!"

JANET: Yup, 'fraid so.

LEE: I loved that movie! The writing left me waterlogged but hey, you look great in ivy.

JANET: Thank you. Thank you very much. That means a lot to me. *(Beat.)* I like your hat.

LEE: Oh, this old thing?

> *(Removes his hat, revealing a receding hairline.)*

JANET: *(Surprised.)* Oh!

> *(Grabbing her own thighs, then to self.)*

Well...that's not so bad.

LEE: My hat?

JANET: No. Eating alone. I thought I was going to have to eat alone.

SARAH: *(Enters with chair. An aside.)*

The night is young.

(SARAH sits.)

JANET: So Lee, tell me about yourself.

LEE: *(Dramatically.)* I was born on a cold, dark, stormy
night—

SARAH: *(Looking at menu, to self.)* Yada, yada, yada.

JANET: *(To Lee.)* Interesting—

SARAH: *(Suddenly.)* You know what?

(She rises and collects her purse.)

I'm not feeling very well and I think, if you don't
mind, I'm going to head on home.

JANET: (Faking disappointment.) Ohhhhh—

LEE: *(Suddenly rising, concerned.)* I'm sorry. Can I drive you
back?

SARAH: No, I'm okay. You guys stay and enjoy your food.

LEE: I'm taking you home.

*(LEE helps SARAH with her sweater while saying
goodbye to Janet.)*

Janet, I hope to run into you again, sometime.

SARAH: No, Lee. Really. We've ordered appetizers, and I'm
sure Janet would love the raw octopus laced with fish
eggs I ordered. Eat, drink, and be married. I mean,
merry. *(Beat.)* I'm not well. Excuse me.

(SHE exits. LEE remains standing, staring off.)

(Blackout.)

End of Scene

ACT ONE

Scene 12

AT RISE:　　　*Later that night. Lights come up on Sarah's apartment. SARAH is standing holding the cordless phone. She has been crying.*

SARAH: *(Blows nose.)* Come on, Jare. Answer. Answer.

JERRI: *(Voice over.)* Hi there. You've reached us. Leave your number and we'll call you right back.

SARAH: *(Into phone.)* Hey you, are you home? Nope. Nope. Pick up. Where are you? Don't you know, you're always supposed to be there for me, no matter what? *(Beat.)*

I'm fine. Really. I know I probably sound really bad, but I'm not. I'll talk with you tomorrow.

(Hangs up phone.)

Okay, Lauren's got a family.

(Dials again.)

She's always home. Come on chick. Come on.

(Beat.)

LAUREN: *(Voice over.)* Howdy!

SARAH: Great.

LAUREN *(Voice over.)* This is the home of the Johnson's— Mister, Misses, Jim, John, Jamie, Joe, and Jeff. At the sound of the beep, beep yourself.

SARAH: Hey youuuu. Gone, huh? Well, it's me, Sarah. Just thought you might be home to help me through one of those really shitty nights.

44

(Quickly covering.)

Schmitty. Schmitty nights. My friend, Schmitty is coming over tonight.

(Giving up the cover.)

I'm sorry, kids. I'm fine, Lauren. Don't worry. Talk to you…whenever.

(Hangs up phone.)

Janet!

(Dials.)

What am I doing?

(Hangs up.)

I know where she is.

(Thinking. Pause.)

No, I can't. Where's my list?

(SHE looks around the apartment but without commitment.)

Where's my list of awful things?

(SHE paces the floor and talks with herself.)

No, Sarah. Listen to me. If you're not going to listen to yourself, listen to me. You are not going to call that man. Remember? Remember what you promised yourself? Put the phone down, now. NOW!

(Responding to herself.)

Okay, okay.

(SHE hangs up phone.)

Now, sit down and have a stiff shot of whiskey.

(Retrieving bottle from kitchen, she sits on couch.)

I don't feel like a drink.

(Beat, talking to herself.)

DRINK. Have a DRINK!

(Fixes herself one and shoots it down.)

I want to call David.

(SHE decides what to do.)

Okay, this is what I'm going to do. I'm going to call him and if he answers I'll ask him over. If he doesn't, I'll hang up and it won't be "meant to be."

(Beat.)

I'll leave it up to God.

(Dials, listens quietly. HE obviously answers.)

Oh, hi. Fine. What are you doing? Nothing? Oh, listen, would you like to come over? I'm really missing you. I'm sorry. I know I shouldn't but I do.

(Beat.)

Really? How quickly can you be here? Great. I'll leave the door cracked. Okay. Bring some popcorn. We'll watch a movie. I love you, too. Thanks, hon. Hurry. Okay. Bye-bye.

(SARAH walks over to the door, opens it a crack, and then turns to walk away when she is overcome with defeat. SARAH slowly slides down the open door, closing it.)

(Blackout.)

End of Act One

ACT TWO

Scene 1

AT RISE: *The following day, in SARAH's apartment. SARAH is sitting left of the table, facing her judgment. JERRI is standing opposite her, justifiably upset.*

JERRI: You did WHAT?!!!

SARAH: You weren't home. No one was home.

    (Pointing upwards.)

    It's God's fault.

JERRI: God had nothing to do with it.

SARAH: Oh, sure, blame me.

JERRI: Sarah! What are you…?!

    (Takes a breath.)

    I don't know what to say.

SARAH: I'm sorry.

JERRI: *I'm* sorry. I'm sorry for YOU.

SARAH: We talked, you know. We didn't just slam the salami.

JERRI: And what did you talk about? The weather? Nothing's changed, has it?

SARAH: Three years is not something to just give up on.

JERRI: Three years and you shouldn't be talking about the weather.

SARAH: I'm not good at this. I need physical love and attention.

JERRI: Well, if that's all you're missing, there's other ways, you know. You shouldn't have called him.

SARAH: You've got it easy, you know that? You've got a nice place and a kind husband who loves you and takes good care of you. I live in this shit hole studio freakin' apartment. I shouldn't swear so much. Does it bother you when I swear?

JERRI: *(Pushing on.)* Relationships are hard, Sarah. You've got to work at them.

SARAH: *(Rises, crosses left.)* Stop telling me that! Crap! I wish everyone would stop telling me that. I'm actually starting to believe it. I've worked very hard at this, and it's not enough. Hard work is not enough!
(Beat.)
You talk to me as though I've planned all of this. That's how you talk to me. Do you know how that makes me feel?
(Silence.)
I did not plan this, Jerri. My life is not a restaurant, and David is not an item on the carefully thought-out menu. If I planned this menu I would have ordered something entirely different. Do you understand that? Some things in life we must just…try to deal with. I'm not someone who just sends back my food if I'm not happy with it. I try, instead, to get it right. I ask to have it heated up. I add a little salt. I try to wash it down with some water.

JERRI: Yeah, but after all that, you've got to remember that a slice of ham is still just a slice of ham. It never suddenly changes into steak—never. Unless, of course, it wants to, and even then, it will always be just a slice of ham.
(Beat.)

A THIN slice, I might add.

SARAH: You're right.

>*(Sits in the left chair.)*

>I know you're right.

JERRI: *(Picking up phone with note attached.)*

>You didn't read the note?

>*(Holding the phone up to Sarah.)*

>What does the note say?

SARAH: *(Reading the note.)*

>"Don't call David."

JERRI: What about the list? You were supposed to read the list of crummy things he's done to you?

>*(Starts to look for Sarah's list.)*

SARAH: *(Rising.)* I looked for it everywhere, and I couldn't find it.

>*(JERRI easily finds the note on Sarah's dresser.)*

>Except there. I didn't look there.

JERRI: Did you try the whiskey I brought you?

SARAH: I don't have a toothache, you know. My whole chest cavity feels like it's going to cave in, and you're suddenly my dentist! You can't numb this kind of pain.

JERRI: What am I going to do with you?

>*(She crosses to Sarah.)*

SARAH: Just don't go drilling, okay? You'd be very dangerous with a drill.

>*(JERRI embraces SARAH. SARAH starts to cry.)*

>I'm lost, Jare. I am truly lost.

JERRI: *(Crosses behind SARAH and kneels to her left. SHE takes Sarah's hands.)*

You know, we've been friends for a very long time, Sarah, and I'm really glad about that. I've known you at lots of different times in your life. I've seen your brilliance. I know your strength. You may not know this now, but you are going to get through this.

(Beat.)

I just can't do it with you.

(The following lines overlap.)

SARAH: What?

JERRI: You're going to have to do this on your own now.

SARAH: Jare?!

JERRI: I don't mean that I don't love you or anything. I just can't keep going through these breakups with you.

(Crossing right.)

You tell me all these things, these horrible things he does, and then I've got to stand by and watch you go back to him.

(Her voice cracks.)

SARAH: All right. Okay. I just won't tell you anymore.

JERRI: He's not good for you, and I can't keep saying it over and over and over again—

SARAH: I'm sorry—

JERRI: Now, I wouldn't mind normally. I wouldn't mind that rollercoaster ride, and I haven't in the past. Don't think that—

SARAH: This is awful.

JERRI: It's just that right now, I'm not in a very strong place myself—

SARAH: Jare?

JERRI: And I think this will be good for you. I really do. You've got to find that strength of yours again, feel it

running through your veins, and finally let go of any
cholesterol that doesn't serve you. That isn't good.
Bad meat—it's just bad meat.

SARAH: Jeez.

JERRI: You're not crazy, and it's not you, and yes, there is
right and wrong. Okay? I've covered all my bases. It's
up to you now.

SARAH: *(Rises and crosses to Jerri.)*
I'm sorry. I had no idea.

JERRI: It's okay. I'm fine. You'll be fine.

SARAH: Yeah.
(Beat.)
Right.

(Blackout.)

End of Scene

ACT TWO

Scene 2

AT RISE: *The next day, in SARAH'S apartment, SARAH and LAUREN are sitting at the table. The phone is lying on the table. SARAH is staring at the phone, and LAUREN is staring at SARAH.*

SARAH: *(Silence.)* So, I just call him up, right? Just make the call.

LAUREN: Right.

(SARAH picks up the phone and freezes).

But it's going to take you actually dialing the phone to do it.

SARAH: Okay.

(Lifts phone again.)

Sit over there. You're making me nervous.

LAUREN: Okay.

(Rises, sits on the couch.)

SARAH: *(Dials phone. Waits, then...)*

Hey, you're home. What are you doing? Cool.

(Beat.)

It's Sarah. Yeah.

(Continuing bravely.)

Listen, I know it's kind of late notice, but...

(Suddenly.)

Could you come over for dinner tonight?

(Surprised.)

Really?! Great. Oh, umm, nothing specific.

(Side glance to Lauren.)

There's just something I'd like to talk with you about.
Cool. See you at…seven? Great. Wine would be great.
No, I've got some candles. Thanks. Seven? See you
then.

(SHE hangs up.)

LAUREN: Well…?

SARAH: You heard.

(Beat.)

He's coming.

LAUREN: And soon, you will be.

SARAH: Lauren!

LAUREN: Great. This is great.

SARAH: *(Correcting her.)*

Good.

LAUREN: *Very* good.

(Beat.)

Now, don't forget to look down.

SARAH: Look down?!

LAUREN: His feet, Sarah. Look at his feet.

SARAH: I'm not going to be looking at his feet.

LAUREN: I cannot begin to tell you how exciting this is for
me.

SARAH: He hasn't said, "Yes."

LAUREN: First things first. Now, let's make up that list of
questions.

(Beat.)

Paper?

SARAH: In the drawer.

(Crosses to couch.)

LAUREN: Oh, goody!

> *(Getting clipboard with pen and paper from drawer.)*
> Now, remember what we talked about.
> *(SARAH nods. LAUREN sits.)*
> You just read off the list and if he can answer each and
> every question with those three, very special letters.
> Namely Y, E, and S—

SARAH: *(Stopping her.)* Lauren, I want you to know
> something. I really appreciate you, you know—your
> friendship. I know how these things can really put
> pressure on a relationship, and you've…well, you've
> always been there for me.

LAUREN: Not a problem.

SARAH: I just want you to know that if you ever get tired
> of…doing this…you know… That I would really be
> understanding with that. Okay?

LAUREN: *(Lovingly letting her off the hook.)*
> Are you kidding me? You actually think I'm here for
> *you?!*
> *(Laughs.)*
> This is for me, babe. I'm living vicariously through
> every move you make. We're just getting to the good
> part now so if you think I'm leaving, you've got
> another "think" coming.
> *(THEY smile at each other and hug.)*

SARAH: Thank you, my friend.

LAUREN: This is great. I'm very excited for you. See? My
> palms are sweating.
> *(Preparing to write.)*
> Number one—

SARAH: He's just coming to dinner—

LAUREN: *(Writing out the list.)*

"Have you been recently tested for—?"

SARAH: It's not like he's said, "Yes."

(Blackout.)

End of Scene

ACT TWO

Scene 3

AT RISE: *That evening, SARAH'S apartment. In the blackout, DIRK has replaced LAUREN on the couch. He has his legs crossed and is gently bouncing his 15-sized foot up and down. SARAH is slightly distracted by this but manages to continue with the business at hand. A bottle of wine and two glasses rests on the table. SARAH is holding the clipboard, and they have just finished the interview process.*

DIRK: Yes! Of course. Anything to help.

SARAH: Oh, Dirk, that would be great! Thank you.

       (In her excitement, SARAH touches DIRK'S hand. There is an awkward moment.)

DIRK: Sure. That's what friends are for.

       (Interpreting the touch as a "pass," DIRK takes SARAH'S feet and moves them up onto the couch, and begins to stroke her leg.)

       That's what friends are for.

SARAH: Right.

       (Stopping him with her voice to make certain all bases are covered.)

       Now, what about your girlfriend—Amelia?

DIRK: Amelia? Oh, no. Don't worry about that. I don't mean it's not a big deal what you're asking, but… No,

Amelia's fine. We break up every other week, and we don't really have the kind of relationship to worry about.

(HE returns to stroking Sarah's leg.)

SARAH: So, she sees other guys as well?

DIRK: No. I don't think so. She uhhh...

(Thinking.)

Hmmm. I never thought about that. No. I'm sure she... Could you hold on a second?

(He crosses to his phone and picks it up.)

Do you mind?

SARAH: No, go ahead.

(DIRK dials and listens.)

AMELIA: *(Voice over.)* Hello there. You got me...

DIRK: *(To Sarah.)* Answering machine.

AMELIA: *(Voice over.)* You know what to do...

SARAH: *(To DIRK, in a whisper.)* Who are you calling?

AMELIA: *(Voice over.)* Speak slowly and leave a number...

DIRK: The woman "out on the town," so it seems.

AMELIA: *(Voice over.)* Do not assume that I have it on my person...

SARAH: Oh. Well, just 'cause she's not answering doesn't necessarily mean that she's...

AMELIA: *(Voice over.)* And as soon as I am free from whatever it is I happen to be doing...

SARAH: ...doing what we happen to be doing. I mean, she could be out shopping or...shopping...

AMELIA: *(Voice over.)* ...I will call you right back.

(Beeping sound and the message is over.)

DIRK: *(With phone at mouth.)* Shopping. Yeah, sure. Shopping.

(HE hangs up phone and moves on.)

Listen, I'm really sorry about you and Dennis—

SARAH: David.

DIRK: David. David.

(Beat.)

I always thought he was a really nice guy.

SARAH: Yeah. Everybody thought that.

DIRK: *(Clapping hands together.)* So, when do we start?

SARAH: Uh…now, I guess.

DIRK: Now?

(Laugh.)

No time like the present.

(DIRK begins to unload wallet, keys, cell phone, and anything else that could possibly get in his way. As HE sets the phone down on the table, HE quickly glances at it to check for any new messages.)

You know, I was beginning to think I would never have this chance with you. I've thought about it. Believe you me, I've thought about it but… Well, you've always been "in" a relationship and all. But then I heard this intriguing rumor about you and Dennis…

SARAH: *(Watching him disrobe in subtle wonder.)*

David.

DIRK: David! Yes! Sorry!

(Continuing.)

In fact, the other night at the movies when you were sitting next to me, the whole time I'm thinking, 'Jeez, enough with the car crashes already. I mean, could this theatre be any more lit? I like stunts and special effects just like the next guy, but we've got to build up some steam here, folks.

(HE has finished undressing and is now standing in his Calvin Klein, well-fitted boxer shorts, shirtless.)

So. Here we are.

SARAH: Yup.

DIRK: Just you and me, "Rebound Partner."

SARAH: Yup.

DIRK: *(DIRK begins his musical seduction with a very sexy song. He is completely committed to executing this song, but his style takes it way over the top, a rendition that would put Elvis to shame. The producers might acquire the rights to the song "Fever" by Peggy Lee, as written here, but the rights must be acquired. A possible public domain song is the chorus to "Ain't Misbehavin'" by Fats Waller.)*

"Bum. Bum. Bum. Bum. Bum, bum. Burn. Bum. Da, da, da, da."

(HE moves slowly toward his victim, snapping his fingers to the beat.)

"Never know how much I love ya'. Never knew how much I cared."

(Puts arms around Sarah's waist.)

"When I put my arms around ya', you give fever that I want to share. You give me fever..."

(HE unzips her skirt and lets it fall, leaving Sarah in her half-slip with the skirt around her ankles.)

"...when I touch you. Fever all through the night. Fever!"

(Pulls her shirt up over her head, leaving her bound at the wrists as though she has just been held up. DIRK quickly glances down at her breasts.)
"I'm on fire. What a lovely way to burn."
(DAVID goes in for the kill as we hear his cell phone on the table vibrate.)

(Blackout.)

End of Scene

ACT TWO

Scene 4

AT RISE: *LEE and SARAH are back sitting at the table DSR, another fine dining restaurant. THEY have been given their drinks, SARAH has a cocktail and LEE a soda.*

SARAH: Lee?

LEE: Yeah?

SARAH: What do you look for in a woman?

LEE: Long legs.

SARAH: What else?

LEE: What they can lead to.

SARAH: Every woman has that.

LEE: Oh yeah? Did you see "The Crying Game?"

SARAH: I'm serious now.

LEE: I don't know, Sarah—compatibility. What's up with you tonight? You seem...ponderous.

SARAH: Ponderous. Why?

LEE: It means, "Mind off thinking about things."

SARAH: I know what it means. I'm asking why you think I'm...that way?

LEE: Oh, I don't know. You seem a little...off. I prefer you "on."

SARAH: On top?

LEE: I didn't say that.

SARAH: *(Sadly.)* No, you didn't, did you?

LEE: *(Directly at her.)* No, I didn't.

(Pause.)

SARAH: Are you going to tell me or not?

LEE: What?

SARAH: About the other night.

> *(Pause.)*
>
> Janet!

LEE: Oh! Is that why you're—?

SARAH: Ponderous?

LEE: Yes.

SARAH: No.

LEE: Oh. Okay.

SARAH: Well???

LEE: I don't do that. I don't tell things about things that go
    bump in the night.

SARAH: Did things so "bump in the night?"

LEE: What's up with you?

SARAH: I don't know. I'm sorry.

> *(Beat.)*
>
> I guess I was just wondering if actresses pet on the
> first date?!

LEE: Sarah, nothing happened. I don't know why I'm telling
    you this because it truly is none of your business—

SARAH: None of my business?

LEE: None of your business.

SARAH: Of course, it's none of my business because you're
    my "friend!"

LEE: This is the first time you've had alcohol in my presence,
    and I must say, I don't like the effect it has on you.

SARAH: It's not the alcohol.

LEE: What is it then?

> *(HE gasps.)*

Oh my God!

SARAH: What?

LEE: I don't know why I haven't picked up on this before.

SARAH: What?

LEE: Why, it's written all over your face.

SARAH: What?

LEE: This is your time of the month, isn't it?

SARAH: What?

LEE: You're menstruating, aren't you?

SARAH: No!

LEE: I'm kidding.

SARAH: Thank God.

> *(Pause.)*

LEE: *(Empathically putting it together.)*
> So, how long have you been broken up?

SARAH: One and a half weeks.

LEE: Ohhhhh. You're rebounding.

SARAH: What?

LEE: Rebounding—hitting on all the men in your immediate
> circle.

SARAH: Hitting on all the men—?

LEE: *(Explaining.)* When two people break up there's this
> thing that happens. They call it—"The Rebound." So
> and so's on "The Rebound."

SARAH: I know what rebounding is.

LEE: I don't think you do because everyone refers to it as an
> *emotional* response, but I've gone through it, and I've
> watched other people go through it, and I actually
> think it's *physiological*.

SARAH: Really?

LEE: Oh, yeah.

(Pulling a small dictionary out from his
back pocket.)
Let's see what Webster has to say.
(Begins to look up the word.)

SARAH: *(Bewildered.)* Where did you pull that out from?

LEE: *(Searching.)* "Rebel...Rebirth..."
(Looking up.)
Do you mind?

SARAH: Sure.

LEE: *(Reading.)* "Rebound. Number one: to spring back after
striking another body. Number two: to recover, as
from ill health or discouragement."
(Looking up.)
Getting closer. "Number three: an instance of seizing
the ball off the backboard or rim, i.e. basketball." Here
we go. "Number four: on the rebound. In an attempt to
replace a recently lost relationship, esp., a romance."

SARAH: Hmmm.

LEE: Sorry. Webster is not at his best here.
(Putting book back into pocket.)
I often find him not wanting to commit to anything
deeper than a simple description and some words he
won't take on at all. Like Bastard-toad-flax, for
example.

SARAH: Bastard...what?

LEE: Bastard-toad-flax. It's a flower.

SARAH: If you know what it is, why do you have to look it
up?

LEE: It's a test of Mr. Webster's omnipotence. Anyway, he
doesn't go deep enough here. "Rebounding" is a very
serious matter. Your body goes into a state of panic

because it is still wanting the things that it has been
having over the past…what? Three years you'd been
with him—David?

SARAH: Yeah.

LEE: Let me ask you something.

(Beat.)

Are you bouncing off the walls?

SARAH: Yup.

LEE: Not able to sleep at night?

SARAH: Yup. I mean, nope.

LEE: Losing weight?

SARAH: Yup.

LEE: Horney as hell?

SARAH: How'd you know?

LEE: You're rubbing up against my leg.

SARAH: Oh, I'm sorry. I thought that was the table leg.

(Beat.)

Sorry.

LEE: It's okay.

SARAH: That's embarrassing.

LEE: I'm sorry you felt like you couldn't talk with me about
it.

SARAH: Well, you know—

LEE: No, I don't.

SARAH: You're a guy. I'm a girl.

(Beat.)

Lee, you're not going to believe what I've gone and
done.

LEE: Try me.

SARAH: Well, you know how, like in today's world, you can't
really afford to…fool around?

LEE: Yeah?

SARAH: Yeah.

LEE: I'm going to need a little more than that.

SARAH: Well, I actually asked a guy-friend of mine if he
would act as my...

(She blows out a breath.)

...my uh...male counterpart.

LEE: Lover?

SARAH: Yes. Lover. Just till I get through this...stage...
whatever it is.

LEE: Rebound.

SARAH: Yes.

LEE: Who's the lucky guy?

SARAH: You don't know him.

LEE: And how long is this going to take?

SARAH: Umm. Well, my uh... boy... ex and I agreed to take
two months off, so...if I can break the habit of him in
that time then...I'm home free.

LEE: So...we're talking six and a half more weeks with this
guy-friend? More or less?

SARAH: Yup.

LEE: Hmmm.

SARAH: What?

LEE: Just thinking. Watching myself and thinking.

SARAH: You're judging me, aren't you?

LEE: *(Honestly.)* No, I'm not.

SARAH: You're looking at me and thinking I'm some kind
of—

LEE: Prostitute?

SARAH: Yeah.

LEE: No, but here. Maybe I can find that waiter who wanted
       your phone number.
       (LEE lifts up his arm to flag down a waiter.
       SARAH stops him playfully.)
       I'm just sorry you didn't ask me.
SARAH: Ask you?
LEE: Yeah. Why didn't you?
SARAH: I thought... Well, the towel story. I thought you
       wouldn't do it.
       (Pause.)
       Would you have?
LEE: Now you'll never know.

       (Blackout.)

End of Scene

ACT II

Scene 5

AT RISE: *Sarah's apartment, early evening. LAUREN*
has just stopped by to catch up on the latest.
BOTH women are sitting on sofa and are in
mid-conversation.

SARAH: It went okay.

LAUREN: How okay?

SARAH: He's coming over again tonight.

LAUREN: Oh my God. When?
          (Looks at watch.)

SARAH: Not till seven. It's okay. The food's already on.
          (Exits to the kitchen to check on food.)

LAUREN: So, we've got a few minutes. Tell me. What
          happened? Quick.

SARAH: (Reentering with a bowl of nuts, she puts them *on*
          the table. SARAH lights the candles.)
          Well, "quick" is what happened.

LAUREN: *(Disappointed.)* Ohhh.

SARAH: It's not that I want some drawn-out session, but it's
          not just the sex I'm missing. My body seems to
          miss...uh...you know.

LAUREN: *(Bluntly.)* No, I don't.

SARAH: "Hangin' out" time. You know, like watching TV
          together, preparing meals together, lying in the
          hammock—

LAUREN: *(Almost disgusted.)* "...together."

SARAH: Yeah. I think that's the kind of thing that builds it up for me.

LAUREN: How were his feet?

SARAH: *(Beat.)* You know, I'm surprised I never noticed them before.

LAUREN: *(Eyes widen.)* Really?

SARAH: Uhah.

(The women sit there. SARAH tries to find the words but can't. Both of them, satisfied with no words, sit in silence, almost not breathing.)

LAUREN: Could you get me a glass of water?

(Beat.)

Sarah?

SARAH: Oh.

(SHE rises and crosses to kitchen and returns with glass.)

LAUREN: *(Drinking.)* So, did he bring his test results?

SARAH: *(Beat.)* I felt so stupid about that.

LAUREN: Did he?

SARAH: Yes, I got it, and I gave him mine, but I kept thinkin', I'm making all these demands on this guy, and what am I offering him in return?

LAUREN: What are you offering him?! What are you offering him?! Sex!!! That's what you're offering him. Not to diminish any beautiful, sweet, innocent thoughts you may still entertain in that angelic head of yours…

(Rises and crosses above table.)

…but this setup is a man's fantasy; I mean, come on. You're offering him sex!

(As an afterthought, looking at table.)

…and dinner. Hell, ya' might as well do him on the table.

(Back to Sarah.)

And you're asking for nothing in return. Nothing! No ties. No calls. No emotional baggage. No meeting the folks. No foreplay. Just plain, honest to goodness—

SARAH: *(Interrupting her.)* I liked that, though. That last… part. There.

LAUREN: Foreplay?

SARAH: Yeah. That's what life is, Lauren—the leading up to things. It's not the thing itself.

LAUREN: *(She begins to eat nuts from bowl.)*

Okay, let's back up here to where Sarah was just a few, short weeks ago. What's your goal? What did we talk about?

SARAH: *(From memory.)* We talked about me creating a situation for myself where I can feel strong, safe, and nourished enough to let go of—

LAUREN: *(Interrupting SARAH.)*

No, no, no. That's not what we said. We said nothing about strong, safe nourishment. We said "physical support." "Physical, sexual support" so you can squeeze yourself, like a bad lemon, out of this unhealthy relationship.

SARAH: *(SHE stands and takes the dish away from Lauren.)*

I'm not a bad lemon just 'cause I don't think like you.

LAUREN: That's not what I meant. Forget about it.

(Beat.)

I'm sorry, Sarah. I didn't mean—

SARAH: *(SHE looks at watch.)* It's seven o'clock. You gotta go.

LAUREN: Let me be here when he gets here.

SARAH: No.

LAUREN: I'll just say hello. Oh please. He's sooo good
looking.

SARAH: No! This is a private affair!

LAUREN: If it's so private, why do I know all about it?

SARAH: You know, it's no wonder men are so messed up with
their boundaries. They get it from women like us!
Look at us. We are the women that are out there,
teaching men how to treat us.

(Crosses to CD player, DSR.)

I deserve everything I get.

(Turns on music. There is a knock on the door.)

LAUREN: *(Running to door.)* I'll get it.

SARAH: No!

(LAUREN swings open the door.)

LEE: Hi. Is Sarah here?

(LAUREN looks at Lee's feet, thinking it's Dirk.)

LAUREN: Your feet aren't big at all.

LEE: Never judge a book by its cover. Sarah here?

LAUREN: Oh, yeah. Hold on. I mean, come in.

(LEE enters.)

SARAH: *(Surprised.)* Lee?

LAUREN: Lee?!

LEE: Lee. Yes.

SARAH: Lauren, this is my friend, Lee.

LAUREN: Friend?

(LEE starts to speak.)

SARAH: *(Jumping in.)* Yes.

LAUREN: She never told me a smidgen about you.

SARAH: Lee, Lauren.

LEE: Nice to meet you.

LAUREN: Nice to meet *you*.

LEE: Am I interrupting you girls?

LAUREN: No, not me. But I think Sarah's got some big plans—

SARAH: Yes, I do. So, Lauren, if you could be on your way, I can find out what Lee needs, and then he can be—

LAUREN: What "Lee needs?" Actually, I'd like to hear this too.

SARAH: Lauren, could you come over here a minute? Please?
(She does.)
Thank you.
(Leads LAUREN downstage to have some privacy.)
I adore you, but this vicarious stuff has reached its limit. I want you to try to be a normal, upstanding woman long enough to say your goodbyes and get your ass out the door. I'll fill you in later.

LAUREN: You will?

SARAH: Yes, I will.

LAUREN: Promise? You've never broken a promise.

SARAH: I promise.

LAUREN: *(SHE kisses SARAH on the cheek quickly, then crosses to the front door with Sarah on her heels.)*
I'm off like a turd of hurdles. It's been very nice meeting you, Lee. What size? 10?

LEE: Twelve.

LAUREN: *(She reacts, "Not bad.")*
I hope your evening is a pleasant one and Sarah, we'll talk real soon.

SARAH: Bye.

LEE: Bye.

LAUREN: *(Turning back in the door frame.)*

        Oh, I'll be home later tonight if you—

        (SARAH shuts the door on LAUREN, mid-sentence.

        LAUREN'S gone. SARAH turns to LEE.)

LEE: *(Calling after her.)* Nice meeting you.

SARAH: Hi.

LEE: Hi.

SARAH: What's up?

LEE: Nothing. Just thought I'd stop by and say hello.

SARAH: *(Waving.)* Hello.

LEE: *(Crosses in, looks around.)*

        I've never seen your place except for the outside when

        I picked you up that first time out for dinner.

SARAH: *(Nervously straightens pillows on couch.)*

        Well, it's kind of a mess right now.

LEE: I disagree. I think it looks great. In fact, it looks like

        you're expecting company.

        (Hovering over the table with candles.)

SARAH: What?

        (Beat.)

        These?!

        (Blows out candles.)

        No. Just burning them to…ward off bad spirits, is all.

        So, what brings you 'round here? I thought you had an

        important writer's conference or something—

LEE: *(Listening.)* Who's that?

SARAH: *(Looks to door.)* What?

LEE: On the radio? Classical station?

SARAH: Oh, no, no. That's um. Hmmm. My mind's drawing

        a blank for some reason...

        (SHE looks at the CD cover.)

Rachmaninoff. Rhapsody. It's my favorite piece.

LEE: *(Taking his time, strolling to center.)*

Hmmm. That's really lovely.

(Listening.)

Really lovely.

SARAH: Glad you like it.

(SHE turns off music and crosses to front door.)

Listen, could we maybe have dinner—

LEE: Dinner? Great.

(HE sits at the table.)

I'm starved.

(HE tucks napkin into shirt.)

SARAH: No, tomorrow night. Dinner tomorrow night.

LEE: No. I'm sorry. I've got big plans tomorrow night. You see, I have this friend who's...in a really bad way. The decisions she's making are not sound ones at present.

SARAH: Lee, I love our times together, but not here.

LEE: You said just the other night that you'd prefer to eat in.

SARAH: Okay, then, not now. I have plans tonight, and my plans started, uh...

(Glancing at watch.)

...some seven-odd minutes ago, so if you'd...

(Going to the door once more.)

LEE: He's not coming.

SARAH: Who?

LEE: Your "guy-friend."

SARAH: Yes, he is.

LEE: Uh...no.

SARAH: And how do you know this?

LEE: I uh...ran into him out on the sidewalk and asked him not to.

SARAH: You what?!

LEE: *(In defense.)* I was a complete gentleman.

SARAH: I'm sure you were, Lee, but... I'm sorry that just
wasn't your place to do that—

LEE: *(Rises suddenly and moves toward her.)*
Sarah, listen to me. I'm not going to mince words.
(Beat.)
I'm your man. I'm the guy. I want you to use me. I
know you may think I've lost my mind, and maybe I
have, but...I'm perfect. Not perfect according to
Webster, but I'm perfect for you...
(Beat.)
I mean, for right now...for what you're going through.
(Beat.)
I did a bad thing tonight, Sarah, but I did it for the
right reasons. I want you to listen to me.

SARAH: I am.

LEE: *(Referring to door.)* I waited outside your door. I guess I
just wanted to see him. I thought it would make me
feel better somehow, but when I saw him, I knew. I
instantly knew he wasn't right. I mean...for now...for
what you're—

SARAH: For what I'm going through.

LEE: Yes. Exactly.
(Beat.)
So, interview me.
(He sits down at the table.)
Ask me the questions you asked this guy. What do I
need to do to qualify?

SARAH: Lee?

LEE: Yeah?

SARAH: You're my friend.

LEE: Yeah, isn't it great?!

SARAH: Yes, but I can't. Uh… I can't ask this of you.

LEE: He was your friend.

SARAH: Yes, but not like you. He was a casual friend.

LEE: A casual friend for casual sex.

SARAH: *(Moving into him at the table.)*
Yes. That's exactly right.

LEE: I can do that. I'm your man. Ask me your questions.

SARAH: Lee…?

LEE: *(Suddenly passionate.)* Please!!!
(Pause.)

SARAH: I'll just grab my clipboard here.
(SHE does, then sits to the right of the table.)
Okay. Number one: "Do you have recent proof of a negative HIV test?"

LEE: Yes. In fact—here. I brought it with me.
(Pulls a sheet of paper from pocket.)
In case, you know—

SARAH: In case you met someone on your way over?

LEE: Ya' never know. I'm a lucky sort of guy.

SARAH: Okay.
(Clears throat.)
Number two: "Can you commit to this 'unique situation' for a period of two months?"

LEE: *(Quickly.)* Yes.
(Beat.)
I can.

SARAH: Okay. Number three: "Can you be 'on call' for moments of emotional and physical breakdown with regard to this 'unique situation.'"

(SHE pauses.)

LEE: "Rebounding." Yes. You bet.

SARAH: Okay.

> *(Sitting up in the chair.)*
>
> Now...number four: "Can you give of yourself completely during this two month..." Actually, Lee, it's only six and a half weeks now—

LEE: Six and a half weeks—

SARAH: Yes.

> *(Continuing.)*
>
> "...and not become emotionally and/or physically attached in any way harmful to the person involved." To me. Harmful to me.

LEE: *(Beat.)* Yes.

SARAH: Okay. Well...

> *(Beat.)*
>
> I feel kind of funny.

LEE: Why?

SARAH: I don't know.

LEE: Did I answer them all correctly?

SARAH: *(Rising and moving away.)*

> You know you did.

LEE: So, what now?

SARAH: You seem to be enjoying this an awful lot.

LEE: Actually, I am. Thank you.

SARAH: I think I need someone who doesn't enjoy it so much.

LEE: Oh yeah, and that makes for really great sex.

SARAH: I think I do!

LEE: Personal enjoyment level was not one of the questions.

> *(As SARAH sits on right arm of couch, LEE rises.*

THEY do this exchange slowly, watching each other.)
What now?

SARAH: I don't know.

LEE: Well, what did you do with him?

(Almost making fun of the name.)
With "Dirk."

SARAH: You know his name?

LEE: *(Referring again to the front door.)*
We had a little conversation out there…on the step.

SARAH: What did you say to him?

LEE: Nothing.

SARAH: Right.

LEE: *(Absentmindedly picks up clipboard from table.)*
I just asked him a few questions of my own.

SARAH: Which were…?

LEE: Where he was from, how you two met, and…why he
had agreed to this "unique situation."

SARAH: And what did he say?

LEE: Los Angeles, in a grocery store, and the rest I'll tell you
after dinner.

(Beat.)
I'm starved.

(Sits in same chair, left of table.)

SARAH: *(Rising and crossing in.)*
You don't want to go out?

LEE: No, you kidding? This is great. You should have asked
me first, Sarah. I would have done it for the home-
cooked meals.

SARAH: *(Crosses to kitchen.)*
Not for my home-cooked meals, you wouldn't.

(Exits.)

LEE: *(Calling after her.)*
      What did you make?
SARAH: *(Offstage.)* Pasta!
LEE: *(Putting napkin in shirt.)*
      Sounds great.
SARAH: *(Entering with pan.)* It's burnt.
LEE: Let's go out.
      (LEE rises, and together THEY blow out candles in a surprisingly timely fashion.)

      (Blackout.)

End of Scene

ACT TWO

Scene 6

AT RISE: *SARAH'S studio apartment, later that evening. LEE and SARAH are sitting across from each other, downstage of the table. The dinner dishes and candles are still present, along with an almost empty jar of oysters. LEE reluctantly digs one out and drops it into his mouth. SARAH does the same. With only two more left, they repeat the ritual, finishing the jar. In swallowing, they are not without the expected facial expressions.*

LEE: Anything yet? Anything at all?

SARAH: Nope. How 'bout you?

    (LEE leaps off his chair, quickly leans SARAH back in her chair, and kisses her passionately. HE then returns to standing position.)

SARAH: *(Continued.)* Wow!

LEE: Just kidding. I thought maybe if I—

SARAH: Pretended?

LEE: *(Sitting back down.)* Yeah.

SARAH: *(Rises.)* Hey! I got an idea!

LEE: *(Guessing and standing.)* Chocolate! I've got some in my glove compartment. Be right back.

    (HE speeds out the front door.)

SARAH: *(To self.)* Actually, that's not what I was going to say at all. Negligee. That's what I was going to say.

(Crosses stage right and looks through drawer.)
Negligee!
(SHE snaps it out of drawer along with the second a item.)
And… double-sided tape!
(Exits into kitchen/bathroom.)
LEE: *(Entering with chocolates, glances around.)*
Hey, where'd ya go?
(Seeing that SARAH is nowhere in sight, LEE passes time by eating one of his chocolates. SARAH enters from the kitchen in a knockout teddy and poses in the door frame.)
LEE: Wow!
SARAH: *(Breaking sexy pose.)*
Yeah? Ya think?
LEE: I've never seen anything quite like it...
(Deadpan.)
…in that color blue.
SARAH: That's it. I quit!
(SHE exits.)
LEE: I'm kidding. You look great, Sarah.
(SARAH reenters cautiously.)
I had no…idea. I mean, I had an idea, but it wasn't as good as your idea, and my ideas can be pretty… darn…good.
(SARAH re-strikes her sexy pose. LEE nervously offers her one.)
Chocolate?
SARAH: Actually, I was thinking we could slip on some music…

(Starts up CD of Rachmaninoff, then crosses to table and moves chair into position.)

…light these candles here...

(SHE does, then crosses to LEE and guides him over to chair.)

…and then I could slowly lower myself onto that "lap top" of yours.

LEE: There you go—speaking to the writer in me.

SARAH: *(Sitting him down, then straddles his lap.)*

How 'bout you be "the writer in me."

(Playing the part of a seductress, she kisses him.)

LEE: Ah…yeah. Okay. I definitely felt something there. Major movement.

SARAH: Really?!

LEE: Gas, I think.

SARAH: Lee?!

(SHE rises.)

LEE: *(HE rises and crosses DSL.)*

This isn't working, Sarah. We should have never gone out to eat.

SARAH: *(Crossing DSR.)*

I know. Mexican food.

LEE: No, not that. It's just... Well... I got back into the "friendship" mode with you, and now I can't get myself out.

SARAH: Well, I don't know what else to do! This is my best outfit! I put double-sided tape on everything.

LEE: *(Genuinely concerned.)*

To cover your…bodice part?

SARAH: Yeah.

LEE: I'm sorry. Chocolate?

SARAH: No. I'm stuffed. I feel like I'm going to explode.
      (Sits in chair, center.)
LEE: Maybe we should just call it a night and go to bed.
      *(HE blows out candles and begins to clear dishes
      from table.)*
SARAH: Go to bed? You mean…like…you sleep over…here?
LEE: *(Casually.)* Yeah.
      (Exits to kitchen.)
SARAH: *(Repositioning her body in chair as LEE passes.)*
      The two of us, in the same bed?
LEE: Oh, so we can exchange intimate bodily fluids, but
      sharing the same bed is out of the question?
      *(Reenters, gathers more dishes, and exits with them
      again.)*
SARAH: It's just that I have this whole plan to get used to
      sleeping alone again. That part has been really hard
      for me.
LEE: *(He enters and points to couch.)*
      Is this your bed?
      (SARAH is lost in thought.)
      Is this where you sleep?
SARAH: Huh?
LEE: Sleep. Saw the logs? Do the cradle?
SARAH: Oh, yeah. Uh-huh.
      *(LEE pulls out the couch, turning it into a bed.
      SARAH gets the pill bottle from the dresser top.)*
      You see, I take these Calms Forte pills from the health
      food store.
      (Crossing DSR of bed.)
      They're for insomnia.
      (Beat.)

Sleeplessness—

LEE: I know what insomnia is.

SARAH: I put three under my tongue half an hour before I go to bed.

LEE: *(Turning to her.)* Sheets?

SARAH: *(Pointing to the kitchen.)* In the closet.

LEE: *(Exits, from off.)* Uh-huh. I'm listening.

SARAH: *(Continuing.)*

And then I read "Charlotte's Web."

(Picks up book from bedside, holds it to her chest.)

LEE: *(Reenters with sheets, begins to make bed.)*

But Sarah, that's the whole point, isn't it? I'm your rebound partner. I can help you adjust to these things. I'm your Calms Forte sleeping pill. I'm your Charlotte's web.

(Beat.)

Let me be your web.

SARAH: Why are you doing this?

LEE: Honest?

SARAH: Yeah.

LEE: Because I can't live with the idea of anyone else doing it.

SARAH: *(After a beat.)* Okay.

(SHE puts pills and book down, and they begin to make up the bed together.)

Which side do you want?

LEE: *(Decisively.)* I'll take the outside.

SARAH: That's where I sleep.

LEE: Why did you ask?

SARAH: Seemed polite.

LEE: Are you asking or not?

SARAH: Okay. Which?

LEE: The outside. I'm the guy. I should sleep on the outside.

SARAH: What's that about?

    (Exits to kitchen.)

LEE: You know—prowlers and stuff. I should sleep between
    you and the prowlers. Between you and the front door.

SARAH: *(Enters and tosses blanket onto bed.)*

    Okay, whatever.

    (Crossing to dresser.)

    You want a t-shirt? I have a couple of over-sized ones.

LEE: Sure. Thanks. I get cold.

    *(SARAH tosses LEE a t-shirt and stands by the light,
    waiting for him to change.)*

    Could you...uh. I'm sorry, Sarah, could you turn
    around?

    (Beat.)

SARAH: Tell you what. I'm going to get into bed, the inside.
    You turn off the lights, change, and join me…on the
    outside. Okay?

LEE: That sounds good.

    (HE crosses to light switch. SARAH gets into bed.)

    Ready?

SARAH: Yup.

LEE: All right.

    *(LEE turns off the light, but we can still see movement
    of him removing clothes except for boxers, putting on
    a Victoria's Secret t-shirt backward, and then tripping
    while removing shoes. SARAH secretively watches
    from a sitting position in bed.)*

    Ouch.

SARAH: You okay?

LEE: Yeah. Ah. Here we go.

> *(Getting into bed.)*

> Oh man, look out. My feet are cold.

SARAH: *(Settling in.)*

> Well, I'm warm, so keep 'em off of me.

> *(Silence. We hear some tossing, then more silence.)*

LEE: Sarah, should we try that spooning thing or something?

> *(Beat, due to silence.)*

> Maybe?

SARAH: My chest hurts. I feel like I'm gonna cry.

LEE: Oh, really? Here. Let me get the light.

SARAH: No, don't get the light. I don't want to cry in the light.

LEE: *(Rises, crosses to light.)*

> I'm getting the light.

> *(Turning it on.)*

> What's going on?

SARAH: I don't know.

> *(Suddenly.)*

> I feel bloated. You didn't like my negligee, and I haven't shared my bed with someone new in over three years. Ya' know?

LEE: *(Crossing to table.)* I'm sorry.

SARAH: It's not your fault.

LEE: I know. It's just that I'm sorry for you having to go through this.

SARAH: I told you I shouldn't have asked this of you. You're my friend.

LEE: *(To self.)* Friend.

SARAH: It's a whole ordeal now.

LEE: It's okay, you know. I'm fine. I could be sitting home
   alone.
   (Seeing chocolates on table.)
   Eating chocolates.
   *(This unleashes the pain in her heart and SARAH
   begins to cry, slowly at first.)*
   Here, now. Don't cry. Oh, Sarah. Let me get you some
   tissues.
   (Looks around, exits into kitchen.)
   You got any tissues? Ah!
   (Enters with them and sits next to her on the bed.)
   Oh, Sarah? Please don't cry.
SARAH: No, this is good, Lee. This feels really good. This is
   tunnel crying.
LEE: Great. Okay. Well, I'm here. *(Smiling.)* Waiting for you
   at the other end…
SARAH: I know you are.
LEE: …and we've got lots of tissues here. See? We are
   prepared.
   (Pulling them out of box.)
   One, two, three, four, five, six, seven, eight. Eight
   tissues.
   (He kisses the top of her head.)
   I'm right here, and I'm not going anywhere.
   (Kisses her on her cheek.)
   See? Both my arms wrapped around you.
   (Holding her close.)
   Nothing's bigger than me.
   *(LEE kisses SARAH near her mouth, and her
   breathing begins to slow down.)*
   I got ya'.

(Continuing to cradle and stroke her.)
You just go on and cry.
(LEE goes to kiss her once more, but SARAH quietly pulls back. THEY look into each other's eyes and sees something new and surprising and nice. They kiss, ever so slowly. SARAH glances at the light switch on the wall. LEE looks too, then rises and turns off light. SARAH lifts open the covers and lets LEE in. THEY envelop each other.)

(Lights fade out.)

End of Scene

ACT TWO

Scene 7

AT RISE: *Sometime later, in Sarah's apartment. LEE and SARAH are reclining in the bathtub, rolled out, and downstage center.*

SARAH: About a month ago, I was taking a bath, trying to relax because of all that was going on at the time, and I thought, "Boy, it's so great to have a bathtub." You know?

LEE: Yes.

SARAH: I didn't know how much it meant to me. I had gone so long without one.

LEE: I know.

SARAH: I thought if I could just relax, my brain would actually figure out what to do and finally make the big decision. Anyway, I'm lying there, and I see this daddy long leg, or what I thought was a daddy long leg, crawling along the edge of the water inside the tub. And I panicked, I think, because I was naked, and I felt somehow more vulnerable than if I'd been...like wearing flannels and raking leaves in the backyard or something.

LEE: I understand.

SARAH: Anyway, I quickly pulled back and the water swooped forward and pulled the spider down into the tub with me. I felt so bad because his legs were getting all tangled up, you know? So, I grabbed the cream rinse to scoop him out when I realized that he wasn't exactly a daddy-long leg. They're nice. This was some other kind of spider, one I hadn't seen before, but it was just really hard for me to watch. You know? The legs. The beautiful, fragile legs getting all knotted up. *(Beat.)* So I took the cream rinse and scooped him out, watched him untangle himself, and before I knew it, he had crawled from the bottle onto my wrist. I must have been thinking about something else 'cause just then, he bit me. I'd never been bitten by a spider before. I didn't know what to do. I jumped out of the tub and tried to wash him down the drain, thinkin' that would make the bite go away, but he wouldn't go. I started to panic, and it was then I noticed this red line starting to run up my arm. I called the hospital, and they said to come right in. They gave me a shot and everything. It was poisonous. Not majorly so, but enough to cause some problems. Anyway, the point is: I tried to help him—the spider. I tried to help him, and he bit me. I couldn't even get him to go down the drain. *(Beat.)* I've gone my whole life saving spiders, but once you get bitten, you just learn not to go there anymore. *(Silence.)*

LEE: Why are all spiders male spiders?

SARAH: Charlotte's not.

LEE: There you go.

(Blackout.)

End of Play

PROPERTIES

FURNITURE PRESET ONSTAGE

- A pull-out couch that turns into a bed.
- A dresser.
- A small table with two chairs.
- Two other small tables, each with a set of chairs representing different restaurants.
- Bathtub on rollers.

PROPS ON STAGE

- Calms Forte bottle of pills on top of dresser.
- Negligee, double-sided tape, clipboard, paper, pen, address book, and a Victoria's Secret t-shirt are in the dresser drawers.
- Fruit bowl on kitchen table with bananas.
- Phone and candles on table.
- Laminated placemats on the table filled with photographs.
- CD of Rachmaninoff, and CD player.
- Book "Charlotte's Web."

PROPS OFFSTAGE

- 2 bowls of frozen yogurt (mashed potatoes) with plastic spoons.
- Various stuff that Sarah left at David's house.
- A bowl with nuts and a can of soda.
- Sheets, two pillows, and a blanket.
- A box of chocolates.
- A box of tissues.
- Menus from the various restaurants.
- Bottle of whiskey and glass.
- Two cocktails for Lee and Sarah.
- Glass of water for Lauren.
- Jar of oysters.

PERSONAL PROPS

- Lee: Webster's pocket dictionary. Baseball cap, backwards.
- Dirk: Bottle of wine, two glasses, wallet, keys, cell phone.
- Sarah: Watch, cell phone.

AFTER ACT ONE, SCENE 7

- Place note on top of dresser—the list of crummy things.
- Tape note to phone that reads, "Don't Call David."

LISA SOLAND'S PLAYS

AN AFTERNOON WITH SHIRLEY and THE EMPTY
      CHAIR: Complementary One-Act Plays
CABO SAN LUCAS (Samuel French & Smith and Kraus)
THE CHRISTMAS TREE ANGEL RADIO DRAMA
COME TO THE GARDEN (Samuel French)
THE CORPORATE LADDER (Smith and Kraus)
DIFFERENT (Samuel French & Smith and Kraus)
DR. BISCOTTI & THE HUMAN CONDITION
      (All Original Play Publishing)
AN EARTHQUAKE (Dramatic Publishing)
THE HAND ON THE PLOUGH
HAPPY BIRTHDAY, BABY!
HOORAY FOR HOLLYWOOD (All Original Play
      Publishing)
IN THE UPPER ROOM (All Original Play Publishing)
INSPIRED! A Drama With Music (All Original Play
      Publishing)
THE KIND THAT DOESN'T BUDGE (Samuel French &
      Quay Magazine)
KNOTS (Samuel French & Smith and Kraus)
THE LADDER IN THE ROOM (Applause Books)
THE LADDER PLAYS
THE MAN IN THE GRAY SUIT (Samuel French)
MATT & HIS CRAZY WRITING MACHINE (All Original
      Play Publishing)
MEET CUTE
THE NAME GAME (Samuel French)
THE OTHER SHOE (Smith and Kraus)
THE ReBIRTH (Applause Books)
REBOUND AND THE BATHTUB
RED ROSES (Samuel French & Applause Books)
THE SAME THING (Samuel French & Smith and Kraus)
SERGEANT YORK: THE PLAY (All Original Play
      Publishing)
SENSITIVITY (Samuel French)
THE SNIPER'S NEST
SPATIAL DISORIENTATION (Applause Books)
THREAD COUNT (Applause Books)
TRUTH BE TOLD (Samuel French & Quay Magazine)
WAITING (Samuel French, Smith and Kraus, & Applause
Books)

Rebound & the Bathtub is also dedicated to the late Henry Polic II. He lovingly directed a delightful stage reading of the comedy, which was presented at TU Studios on January 21, 2001. The play was produced by The Florida Project & Hilde Garcia, and stage managed by Garfield Mignott. Mr. Polic was a passionate theatre lover and was truly generous with his infinite talent.

What they're saying about
30 SHORT PLAYS
FOR PASSIONATE ACTORS...

"Lisa Soland has here assembled a wonderful collection of short plays. If you're a passionate actor, a teacher or a director looking for a play to do, you won't find a better place to start looking than this book."
— *Lawrence Harbison, Senior Editor, Smith and Kraus & Applause Theatre & Cinema Books*

"Lisa Soland's amazing collection of 30 excellent, sooo entertaining short plays is a must for any would-be playwright, actor or acting group!"
— *Tom Sawyer, novelist, playwright, screenwriter*

"This collection of plays is as varied and eclectic as the human mind itself. They are funny, dramatic, poignant, shocking, outrageous, satirical, imaginative... It's a must-have for writers of short plays and a great resource for theatres that produce them."
— *Peter Colley, playwright, screenwriter, librettist*

What they're saying about
SERGEANT YORK: THE PLAY

"It's simply a wonderful play."
– Deborah York, Executive Director of the Sergeant York Patriotic Foundation and great-granddaughter of Alvin York

"Sergeant York: The Play is... a powerful statement on the nature of war and the power of faith."
– Peter Colley, playwright/screenwriter/librettist

"I thoroughly recommend *Sergeant York: The Play* for any organization seeking an inspirational, wholesome tale of a true American hero."
– Burt Rosen, President and CEO of Knox Area Rescue Ministries Knoxville

"Soland has devoted her significant abilities to share the story of Alvin York's deep personal faith and commitment to Jesus Christ."
– Sam Polson, Lead Pastor of West Park Baptist Church

What they're saying about
DR. BISCOTTI & THE HUMAN CONDITION

"Lisa Soland's *Dr. Biscotti and the Human Condition* is a tour de force and a masterpiece. Its theme centers on nothing less than life's reasons and randomness. Characters represent the fourth dimension—time rather than space. By the end of the play, we learn how life can differ for an array of people, all linked by the interlocutor—their therapist, Dr. Biscotti. This play is original, entertaining, at times shocking, and brilliantly crafted. Dramatically, it has surprises and a wonderful build to a shocking conclusion. I could not get it, or the deep philosophical and sociological issues, out of my head for weeks after seeing it. I am a long-time fan of Ms. Soland, but this is perhaps her deepest play. I would love to see it get all the attention it deserves."
– Andrew Bonime, Feature Film Producer

"Absolutely riveting dialogue and characters. *Dr. Biscotti* is an excellent work. I was absolutely captured by the characters and their stories."
– Steven L. Sears, TV Producer/Writer

www.ingramcontent.com/pod-product-compliance
Lightning Source LLC
Chambersburg PA
CBHW071025120626
46546CB00003B/1215